Rhyming Pairs

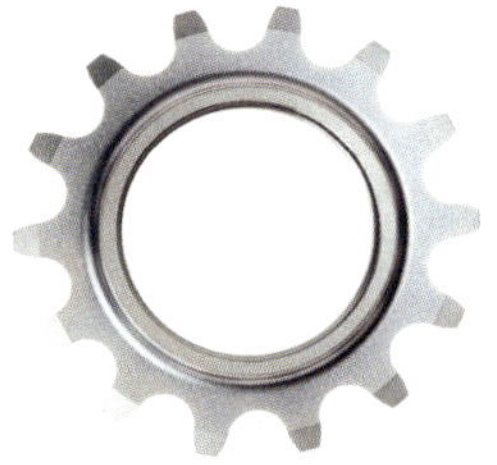

Written by
Stephen Rickard

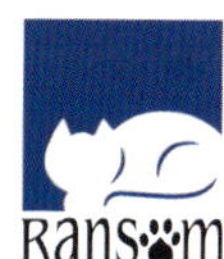

Ransom

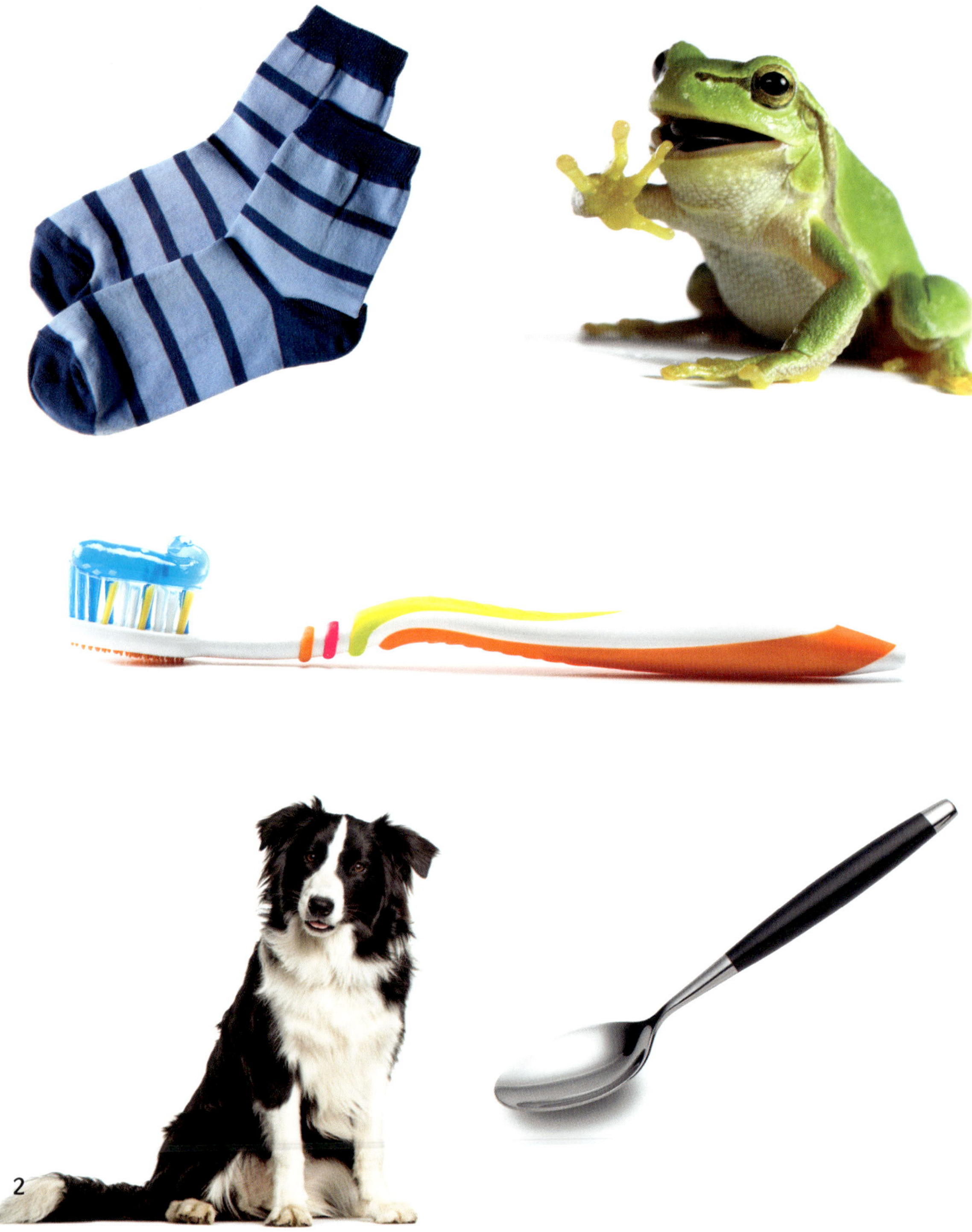

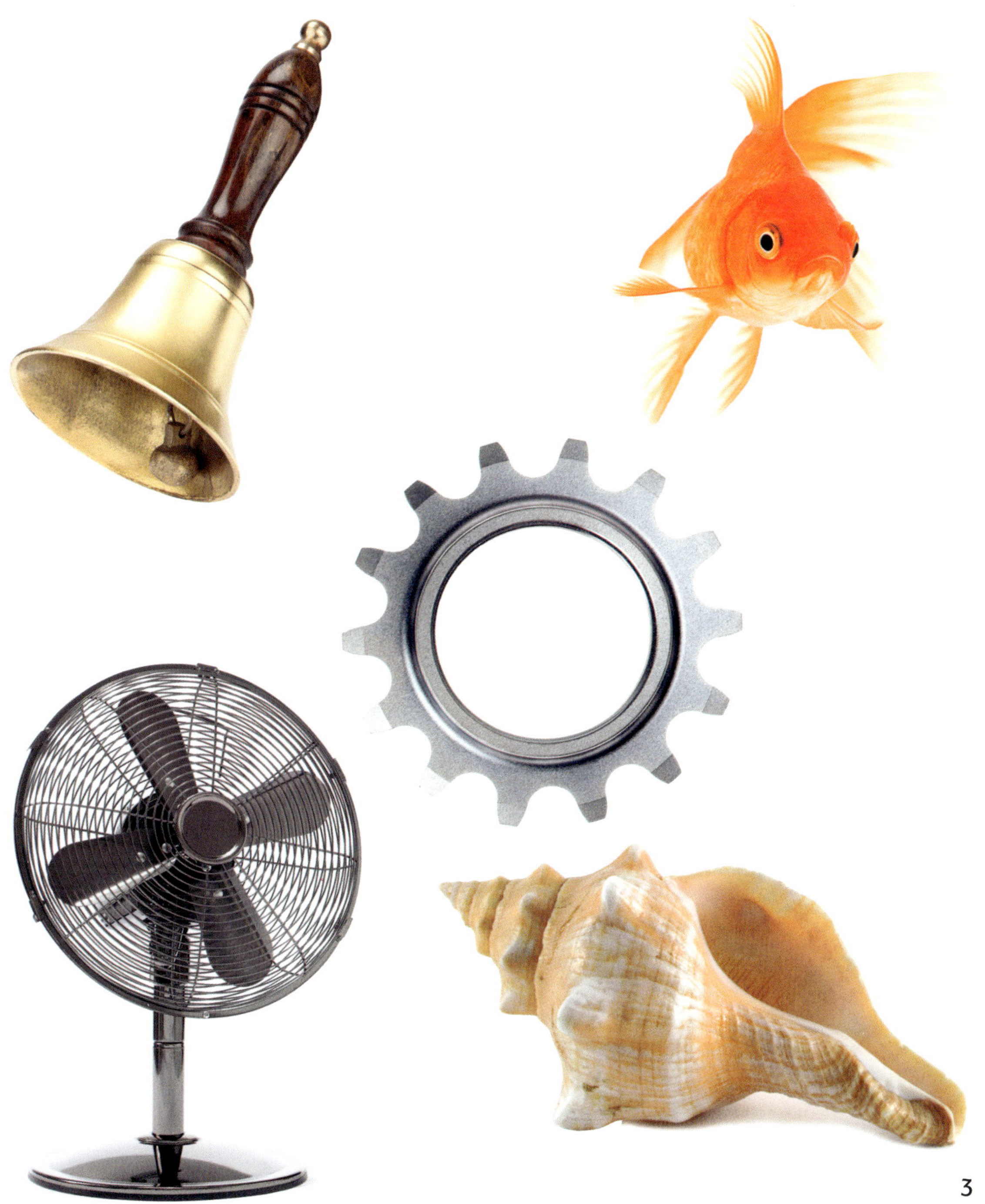

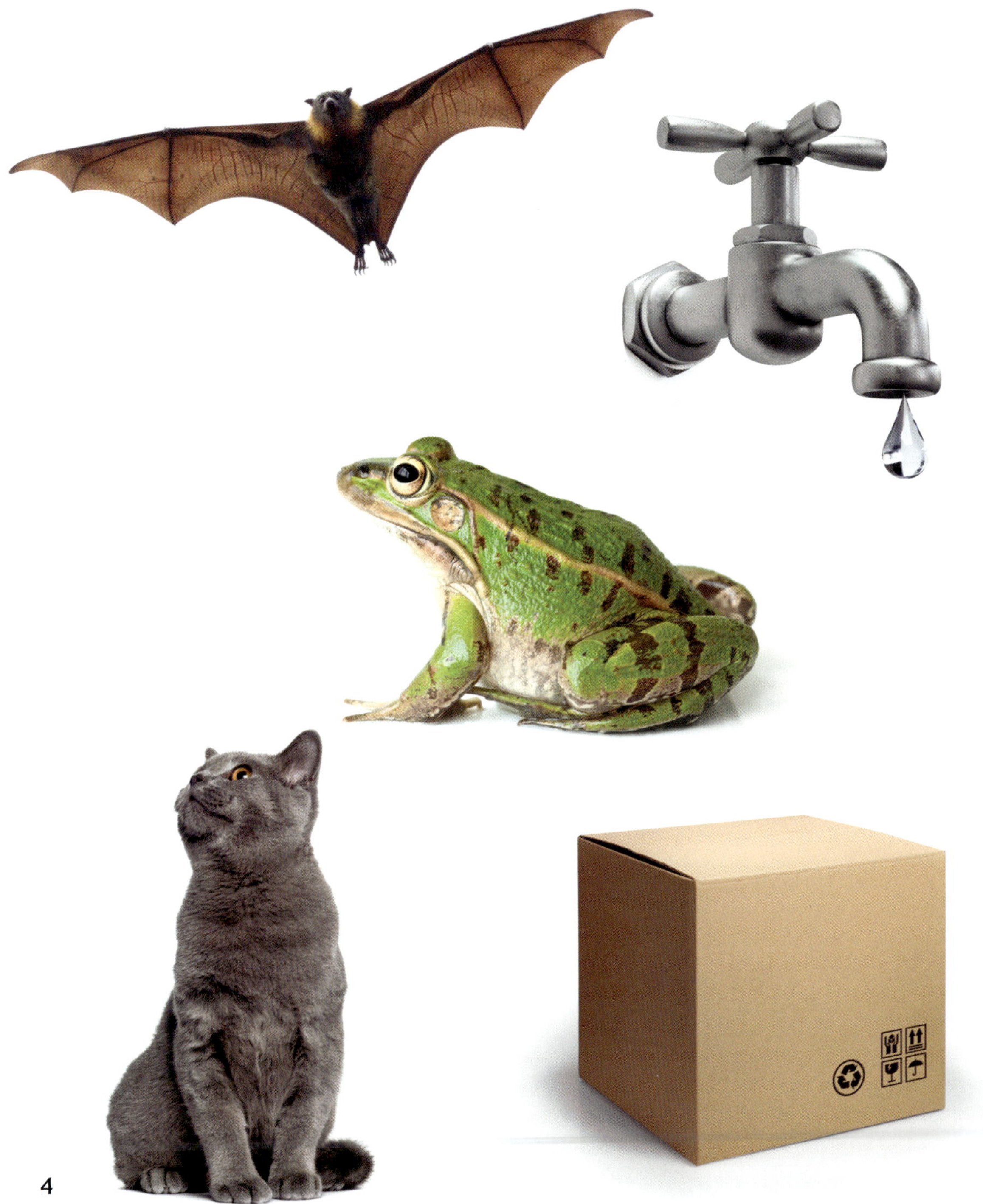

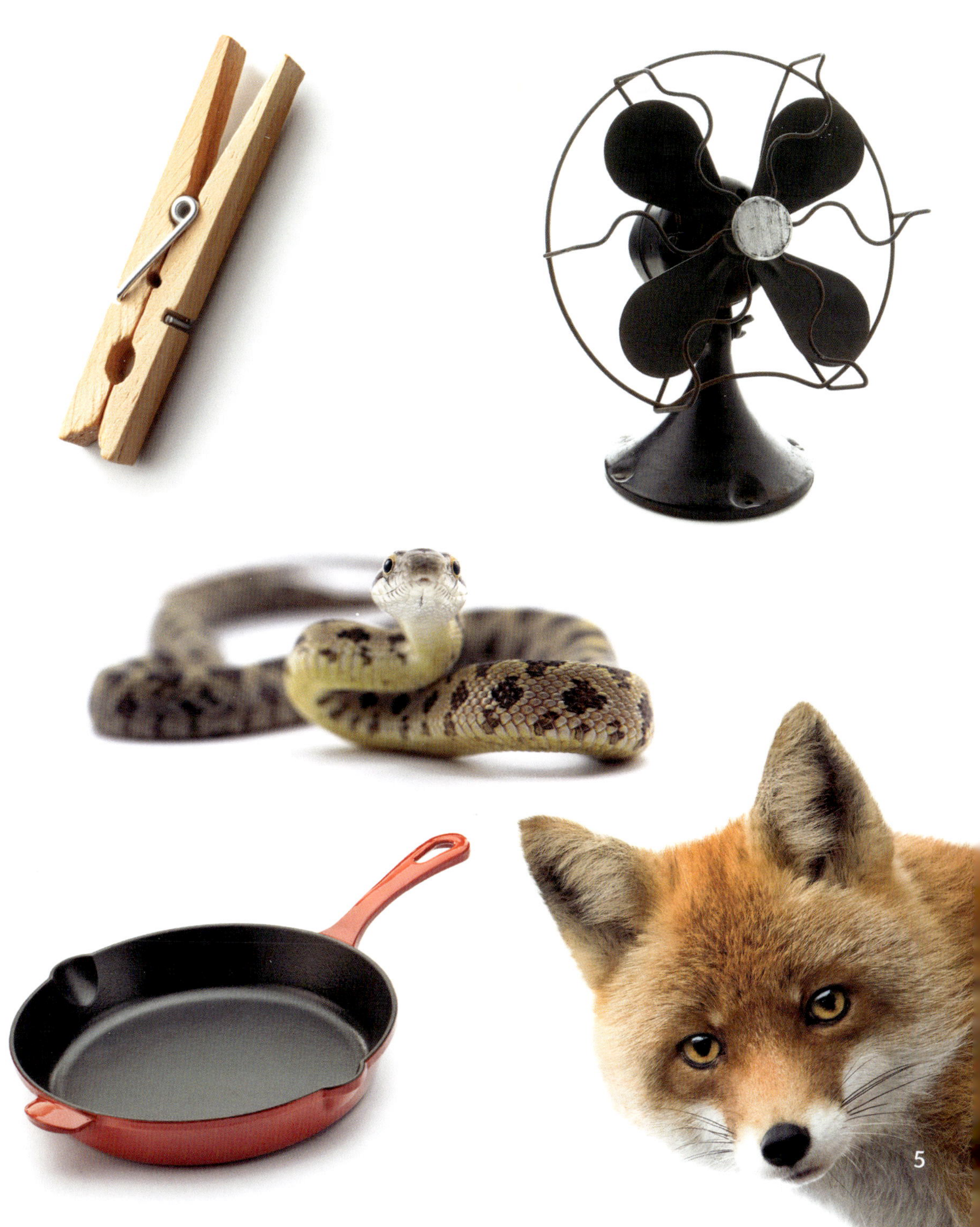

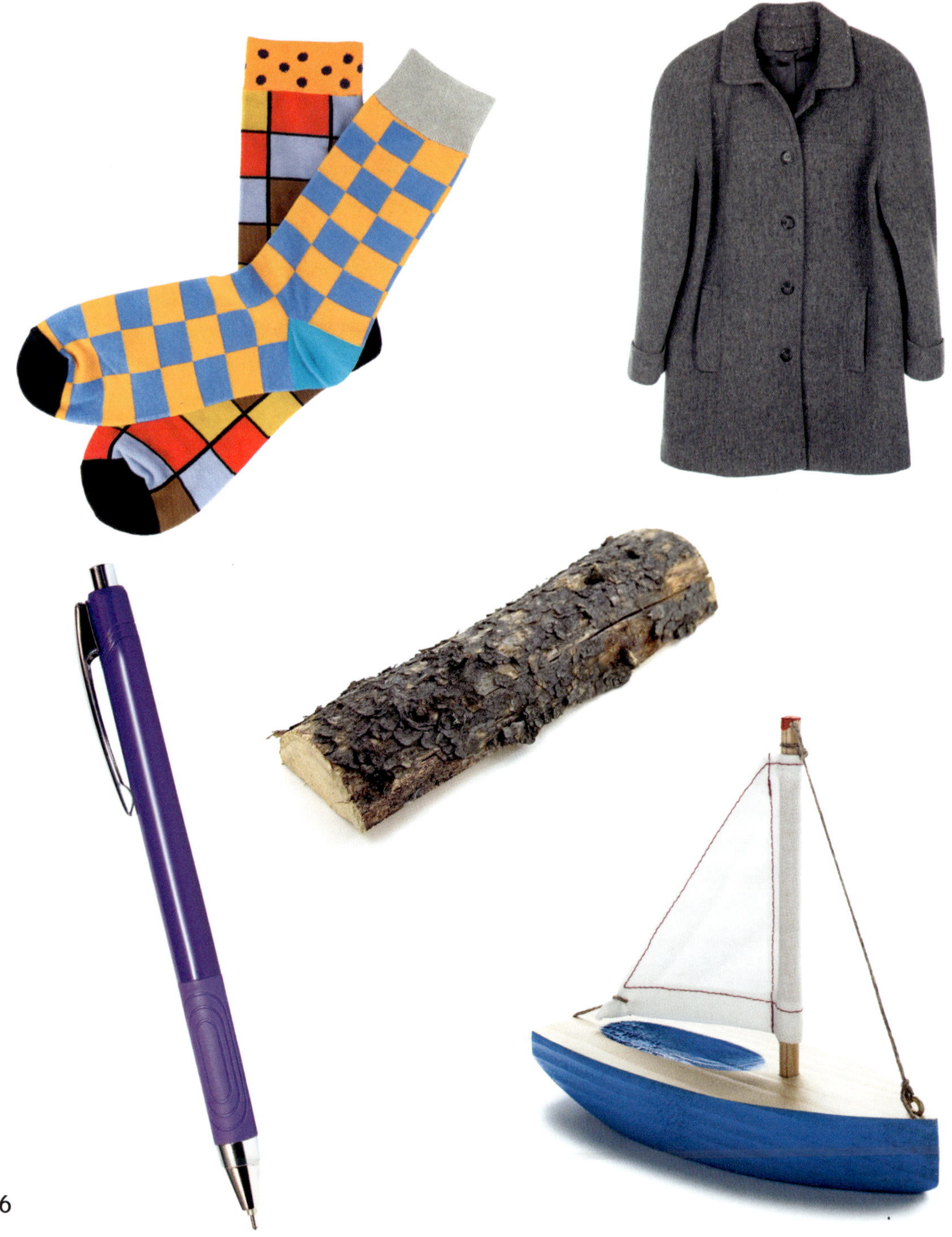

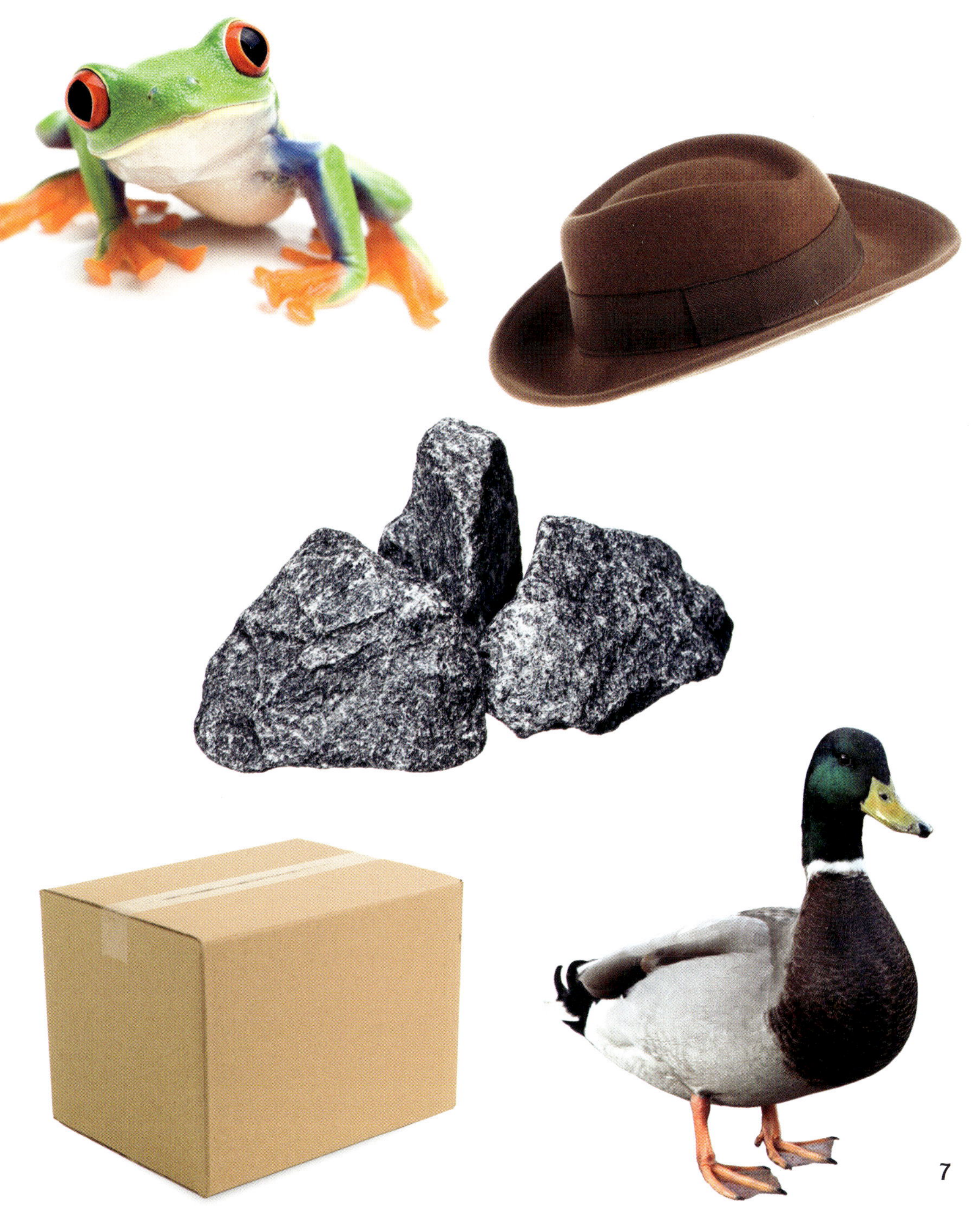

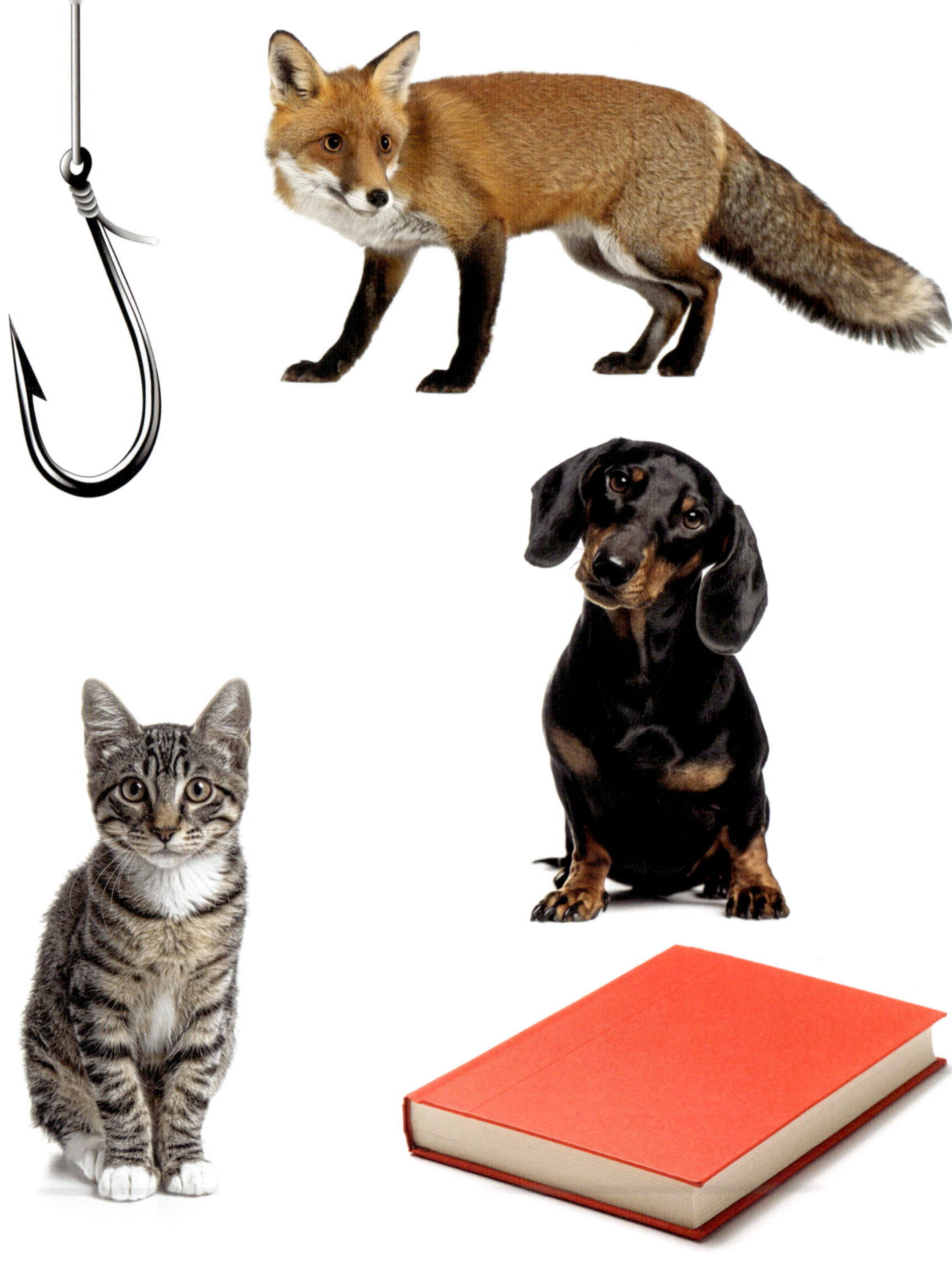